Easy Homemade Cookbook

Discover The Secrets of Over 100 of The Most Delicious and Easy to Cook Homemade Recipes

Laura Rollison

SPECIAL DISCLAIMER

All the information's included in this book are given for instructive, informational and entertainment purposes, the author can claim to share very good quality recipes but is not headed for the perfect data and uses of the mentioned recipes, in fact the information's are not intent to provide dietary advice without a medical consultancy.

The author does not hold any responsibility for errors, omissions or contrary interpretation of the content in this book.

It is recommended to consult a medical practitioner before to approach any kind of diet, especially if you have a particular health situation, the author isn't headed for the responsibility of these situations and everything is under the responsibility of the reader, the author strongly recommend to preserve the health taking all precautions to ensure ingredients are fully cooked.

All the trademarks and brands used in this book are only mentioned to clarify the sources of the information's and to describe better a topic and all the trademarks and brands mentioned own their copyrights and they are not related in any way to this document and to the author.

This document is written to clarify all the information's of publishing purposes and cover any possible issue.

Table Of Contents

Table Of Contents

Table Of Contents

Easy Spinach Lasagna with White Sauce

Ingredients

1 (10 ounce) package frozen chopped spinach
29 ounces Alfredo-style pasta sauce
1/2 cup skim milk
1 (8 ounce) package lasagna noodles
1 pint part-skim ricotta cheese 1 egg
8 ounces shredded carrots
8 ounces fresh mushrooms, sliced
1/2 cup shredded mozzarella cheese

Directions

Preheat oven to 350 degrees F (175 degrees C). Coat a 10x15 inch lasagna pan with cooking spray.

Place the spinach in a medium bowl. Microwave, uncovered, on high for 4 minutes. Mix in ricotta. Beat the egg with a wire whisk, and add it to the spinach and ricotta. Stir well to blend.

Combine pasta sauce with milk in a medium bowl. Mix well.

Spread about 1/2 cup pasta sauce mixture evenly in the bottom of the dish. Place 3 uncooked noodles over the sauce. Spread half of the spinach mixture over the noodles. Sprinkle with half of the carrots and half of the mushrooms. Place 3 more noodles over the vegetable mixture. Pour 1 1/2 cups sauce over the noodles.
Spread the remaining spinach mixture over the sauce, followed by layers of the remaining carrots and mushrooms. Place 3 more noodles over the vegetables. Pour remaining sauce evenly on top. Sprinkle with the mozzarella cheese. Spray a sheet of aluminum foil with cooking spray. Cover the dish tightly with aluminum foil, spray side down.

Bake for 50 to 60 minutes. Remove from oven, uncover, and spoon some sauce over the exposed top noodles. Turn the oven off, and place the uncovered dish back into the warm oven for 15 more minutes. Serve at once, or let rest until ready to serve.

Fast and Easy French Onion Dip

Ingredients

1 1/4 cups nonfat sour cream
1/2 cup fat-free mayonnaise
1/8 cup chopped green onion
1 (1 ounce) package dry onion
soup mix
1/4 teaspoon dried minced onion
salt and pepper to taste

Directions

In a medium bowl, stir together nonfat sour cream, fat-free mayonnaise, green onion, dry onion soup mix, dry minced onion, salt and pepper. Chill until serving.

Easy German Chocolate Cake

Ingredients

1 1/3 cups flaked coconut
1 cup chopped pecans
1 (18.25 ounce) package German chocolate cake mix
1 (8 ounce) package cream cheese, softened
1/2 cup butter or margarine, softened
1 egg
4 cups confectioners' sugar

Directions

Sprinkle the coconut and pecans into a greased and floured 13-in. x 9-in. x 2-in. baking pan.

Prepare cake mix according to package directions. Pour batter into prepared pan.

In a mixing bowl, beat cream cheese and butter until smooth. Add egg and sugar; beat until smooth. Drop by tablespoonfuls over the batter. Carefully spread to within 1 in. of edges.

Bake at 325 degrees for 55-60 minutes or until a toothpick inserted near the center comes out clean. Cool for 10 minutes; invert onto a serving plate.

Fast and Easy Spinach with Shallots

Ingredients

tablespoon olive oil
shallot, diced
(10 ounce) bag baby spinach
leaves
kosher salt and freshly ground
pepper to taste

Directions

In a large skillet, heat olive oil over medium heat. Stir in shallots and cook until transparent, about 5 minutes. Add spinach, sprinkle with salt and pepper; cook and stir 3 to 5 minutes until leaves are wilted and reduced.

Easy Layer Bar Cookies

Ingredients

1/2 cup butter or margarine
1 cup graham cracker crumbs
1 1/2 cups semisweet chocolate chips
1 1/2 cups butterscotch chips
1 1/2 cups flaked coconut
1 cup chopped walnuts
1 (14 ounce) can sweetened condensed milk

Directions

Preheat oven to 350 degrees F (175 degrees C).

Melt the butter or margarine in a 9x13 inch baking pan. Sprinkle the graham cracker crumbs evenly over the butter. Sprinkle on the chocolate chips and butterscotch chips. Cover with the flaked coconut. Sprinkle the walnuts on top of the coconut layer. Finally, pour the condensed milk over everything as evenly as you can.

Bake for 30 to 35 minutes in the preheated oven. Cool, and cut into bars.

Easy Beef Goulash

Ingredients

1 1/2 cups uncooked spiral pasta
1 pound boneless beef sirloin steak, cut into 1/8-inch-thick strips
1 tablespoon canola oil
1 medium onion, chopped
1 medium green pepper, chopped
1 (14.5 ounce) can diced tomatoes, undrained
1 1/2 cups water
1 cup reduced-sodium beef broth
1 1/2 teaspoons red wine vinegar or cider vinegar
1 teaspoon paprika
1 teaspoon sugar
1/2 teaspoon salt
1/4 teaspoon caraway seeds
1/4 teaspoon pepper
2 tablespoons all-purpose flour
1/4 cup cold water

Directions

Cook pasta according to package directions. Meanwhile, in a large nonstick skillet, stir-fry beef in oil for 4-5 minutes or until browned. Add onion and green pepper; cook and stir for 2 minutes. Stir in tomatoes, water, broth, vinegar and seasonings. Bring to boil. Reduce heat; cover and simmer for 15 minutes. In a small bowl, combine flour and cold water until smooth. Add to skillet. Bring to a boil; cook and stir for 2 minutes or until thickened. Drain pasta; stir into beef mixture.

Quick and Easy Stuffed Peppers

Ingredients

2 large red bell peppers, halved and seeded
1 (8 ounce) can stewed tomatoes, with liquid
1/3 cup quick-cooking brown rice
2 tablespoons hot water
2 green onions, thinly sliced
1/2 cup frozen corn kernels, thawed and drained
1/2 (15 ounce) can kidney beans, drained and rinsed
1/4 teaspoon crushed red pepper flakes
1/2 cup shredded mozzarella cheese
1 tablespoon grated Parmesan cheese

Directions

Arrange pepper halves in a 9 inch square glass baking dish. Cover dish with plastic wrap. Poke a few holes in the plastic wrap for vents, and heat 4 minutes in the microwave, or until tender.

In a medium bowl, mix tomatoes and their liquid, rice, and water. Cover with plastic, and cook in the microwave for 4 minutes, or until rice is cooked.

Stir green onions, corn, kidney beans, and red pepper flakes into the tomato mixture. Heat in the microwave for 3 minutes, or until heated through.

Spoon hot tomato mixture evenly into pepper halves, and cover with plastic wrap. Poke a few holes in the plastic to vent steam, and heat in the microwave 4 minutes. Remove plastic, sprinkle with mozzarella cheese and Parmesan cheese, and allow to stand 1 to 2 minutes before serving.

Easy BBQ Bake

Ingredients

3/4 cup barbecue sauce
3/4 cup honey
1/2 cup ketchup
1 onion, chopped
4 skinless, boneless chicken breast halves

Directions

Preheat oven to 400 degrees F (200 degrees C).

In a medium bowl, combine the barbecue sauce, honey, ketchup and onion and mix well. Place chicken in a 9x13 inch baking dish. Pour sauce over the chicken and cover dish with foil.

Bake at 400 degrees F (200 degrees C) for 45 minutes to 1 hour, or until chicken juices run clear.

Candie's Easy Potato and Onion Dish

Ingredients

8 potatoes, sliced
2 large sweet onions, sliced
1/2 cup butter, sliced
1 tablespoon dried parsley
salt and pepper to taste

Directions

Preheat oven to 350 degrees F (175 degrees C).

In a 9x13 inch casserole dish, mix the potatoes, onions, butter, and parsley. Season with salt and pepper.

Bake covered in the preheated oven for 45 minutes, stirring occasionally, or until potatoes are tender.

Easy Raisin Cake

Ingredients

1 cup raisins
2 cups water
1/2 cup butter
1 teaspoon baking soda
1/2 teaspoon salt
1 cup white sugar
1/2 teaspoon ground cinnamon
1/2 teaspoon ground nutmeg
1 cup chopped walnuts
1 3/4 cups all-purpose flour

Directions

Preheat oven to 350 degrees F (175 degrees C). Lightly grease one 10 x 10 inch baking pan.

In a large saucepan boil the raising with the water for 10 minutes. Add the butter or margarine and let cool.

In the same pan add the flour, soda, salt, sugar, cinnamon, nutmeg, and chopped nuts (optional), mix well and pour batter into a lightly greased 10x10 inch baking pan

Bake at 350 degrees F (175 degrees C) for 35 minutes. Serves 8 to 12.

Easy Tortilla Soup

Ingredients

2 (10.5 ounce) cans condensed chicken and rice soup
1 (10 ounce) can diced tomatoes with green chile peppers
1 (8 ounce) can tomato sauce
8 ounces tortilla chips
4 ounces shredded Cheddar cheese

Directions

In a medium saucepan over medium high heat, combine the soup, tomatoes and chilies and tomato sauce. Bring just to a boil and remove from heat. Place some tortilla chips in the bottom of an individual bowl and sprinkle cheese over the chips. Pour soup over the chips and cheese.

Easy Cheesy Cream of Broccoli Soup

Ingredients

(10 ounce) package frozen chopped broccoli

(10.75 ounce) can condensed cream of mushroom soup

1/4 cups milk

8 ounces processed cheese food (eg. Velveeta)

salt and pepper to taste

Directions

Prepare broccoli according to directions. Drain off excess water.

Add cream of mushroom soup and one can of milk to broccoli. Stir and heat thoroughly on low.

Add cheese, stirring until melted. Add salt and pepper to taste. Your quick and creamy soup is ready to serve!

Easy Chocolate Cupcakes

Ingredients

10 tablespoons butter
1 1/4 cups white sugar
4 eggs
1/4 teaspoon almond extract
1 teaspoon vanilla extract
1 1/2 cups all-purpose flour
3/4 cup unsweetened cocoa powder
2 teaspoons baking powder
1/4 teaspoon salt
3/4 cup milk

Directions

Preheat oven to 350 degrees F (175 degrees C). Grease two muffin pans or line with 20 paper baking cups.

In a medium bowl, beat the butter and sugar with an electric mixer until light and fluffy. Mix in the eggs, almond extract and vanilla. Combine the flour, cocoa, baking powder and salt; stir into the batter, alternating with the milk, just until blended. Spoon the batter into the prepared cups, dividing evenly.

Bake in the preheated oven until the tops spring back when lightly pressed, 20 to 25 minutes. Cool in the pan set over a wire rack. When cool, arrange the cupcakes on a serving platter. Frost with your favorite frosting.

Easy Pheasant Casserole

Ingredients

1 (6 ounce) package dry bread stuffing mix
4 tablespoons butter, melted
1 1/2 cups hot water
1 (10.5 ounce) can chicken gravy
1 pound cooked pheasant, cubed
1 (16 ounce) package frozen mixed vegetables
1/4 teaspoon dried thyme

Directions

Preheat oven to 350 degrees F (175 degrees C).

In a large bowl, combine the seasoning packet from the stuffing mix with the butter and water. Stir in the stuffing crumbs until all the liquid is absorbed.

In a separate 2 quart casserole dish, combine the gravy, pheasant, vegetables and thyme. Stir all together well , then spoon the stuffing mix over the top.

Bake at 350 degrees F (175 degrees C) for 45 minutes, or until hot and bubbly.

T's Easy Chicken

Ingredients

1/4 cup olive oil
1/4 cup fresh lemon juice
1/4 cup diced onion
4 skinless, boneless chicken breast halves
1/2 cup sliced fresh mushrooms
1/2 cup diced tomatoes, drained

Directions

Heat oil, lemon juice and onion in a large skillet over medium heat. When onion is tender, add chicken, mushrooms and tomatoes.

Cook over medium high heat for 5 to 7 minutes each side, stirring occasionally, or until chicken is cooked through and no longer pink inside.

Super Easy Rocky Road Candy

Ingredients

3 (7 ounce) bars milk chocolate
with almonds candy (such as
Hershey's® Milk Chocolate with
Almonds)
cup miniature marshmallows

Directions

Place the candy bars in a microwave safe bowl, and cook in the microwave on Low until melted, approximately 5 minutes. Stir and allow to cool enough to prevent the marshmallows from melting when added to the chocolate. Once cool, stir in the marshmallows and pour into a 8x8 inch baking dish. Refrigerate until firm, about 2 hours. Break into pieces to serve.

Quick and Easy Green Chile Chicken Enchilada

Ingredients

4 skinless, boneless chicken breast halves
garlic salt to taste
18 (6 inch) corn tortillas, torn in half
1 (28 ounce) can green chile enchilada sauce
1 (16 ounce) package shredded Monterey Jack cheese
1 (8 ounce) container reduced fat sour cream

Directions

Preheat oven to 350 degrees F (175 degrees C). Lightly grease a medium baking dish.

Season chicken with garlic salt. Arrange in the prepared baking dish. Bake 45 minutes in the preheated oven, until no longer pink and juices run clear. Cool, shred, and set aside.

With metal tongs, char each tortilla half over the open flame of a gas stove burner for about 1 minute, until lightly puffed.

Pour about 1/2 inch enchilada sauce in the bottom of a medium baking dish, and arrange 6 tortillas in a single layer. Top with 1/2 the chicken, 1/3 cheese, 1/2 the sour cream, and 1/3 of the remaining enchilada sauce. Repeat. Coat remaining tortillas thoroughly with remaining enchilada sauce, and arrange on top of the layers. Sprinkle with remaining cheese, and top with any remaining enchilada sauce

Cover, and bake 45 minutes in the preheated oven. Cool slightly before serving.

Easy Asian Baked Chicken

Ingredients

6 skinless, boneless chicken breast halves
1 cup soy sauce
1/2 cup vinegar
1 green bell pepper, chopped
2 (8 ounce) cans sliced water chestnuts, drained

Directions

Preheat oven to 350 degrees F (175 degrees C).

Place chicken in a lightly greased 9x13 inch baking dish. Pour soy sauce and vinegar over chicken, then sprinkle with bell pepper and top with water chestnuts.

Bake at 350 degrees F (175 degrees C) for about 40 minutes or until chicken is cooked through and juices run clear.

Easy Dutch Oven Cheese Lasagna

Ingredients

1 (32 ounce) jar spaghetti sauce
15 lasagna noodles
2 cups broccoli florets
2 cups cauliflower florets
1 cup green peas
1 cup corn
2 cups shredded mozzarella cheese
1 cup shredded Cheddar cheese

Directions

Pour about 1/2 cup of spaghetti sauce into the bottom of a large, cast-iron Dutch oven with lid. Spread the sauce around evenly.

Place down a layer of three lasagna noodles, and spread about 3/4 cup of spaghetti sauce over them. Lay in the broccoli and sprinkle with 2/3 cup of mozzarella cheese. Repeat this layering of noodles, sauce, vegetables, and cheese using the cauliflower, green peas, and corn.

Cover the corn with the last three remaining lasagna noodles, and spread the remaining spaghetti sauce on top. Sprinkle with the Cheddar cheese.

Place the lid on the Dutch oven, and place 12 hot coals underneath and 12 coals on top. Cook for 75 minutes or until noodles are soft and tender. Remove the coals, and allow to stand for about 10 minutes to firm up a bit before serving.

Slow and Easy Beef Stock

Ingredients

0 pounds beef soup bones, cut
nto pieces
water to cover

Directions

Combine the bones and water in a large stockpot. Bring the mixture to a boil. Maintain a low boil for 24 hours, adding water to keep the bones submerged. Remove and discard the bones. Allow mixture to simmer another 21 to 22 hours. Strain the liquid through a fine-mesh colander and return to the stockpot. Bring to a boil and cook until liquid has reduced to about 2 quarts.

Transfer the stock to heat-safe containers; freeze. Once frozen, there should be three easily-discernable layers. Remove and discard the top-most of those three layers. Thaw remaining portion to use.

Easy Skillet Beef and Hash Browns

Ingredients

1 pound ground beef
1 (10.75 ounce) can Campbell's®
Condensed Cream of Celery Soup
(Regular or 98% Fat Free)
1/2 cup water
1/4 cup ketchup
1 tablespoon Worcestershire
sauce
2 cups frozen hash-brown
potatoes
3 slices process American cheese

Directions

Cook the beef in a 10-inch skillet over medium-high heat until well browned, stirring often to separate meat. Pour off any fat.

Stir the soup, water, ketchup and Worcestershire in the skillet and heat to a boil. Stir in the potatoes. Reduce the heat to low. Cover and cook for 10 minutes or until the potatoes are tender. Top with the cheese.

Easy Grilled Chicken

Ingredients

4 skinless, boneless chicken breast halves
1 cup fat free Italian-style dressing
1 green bell pepper
1 red bell pepper
1 zucchini

Directions

Place washed chicken breasts in large sealable bag. Add 1 cup fat-free Italian dressing and close. Let marinate for 5 to 10 minutes.

Cut up peppers into big chunks, and zucchini into big slices. Put into another sealable bag. Coat with leftover dressing.

Grill chicken and veggies over medium heat.

A Good Easy Garlic Chicken

Ingredients

3 tablespoons butter
4 skinless, boneless chicken breast halves
2 teaspoons garlic powder
1 teaspoon seasoning salt
1 teaspoon onion powder

Directions

Melt butter in a large skillet over medium high heat. Add chicken and sprinkle with garlic powder, seasoning salt and onion powder. Saute about 10 to 15 minutes on each side, or until chicken is cooked through and juices run clear.

Easy Platz (Coffee Cake)

Ingredients

cups all-purpose flour
1/2 cups white sugar
teaspoons baking powder
teaspoon salt
/3 cup margarine
eggs, beaten
/3 cup milk
cup blackberries

Directions

Preheat oven to 350 degrees F (175 degrees C). Grease and flour a 9 inch square pan.

In a large bowl, combine flour, sugar, baking powder and salt. Cut in margarine until mixture resembles coarse crumbs. Set aside 3/4 cup of crumb mixture, to be used as a topping for the cake. Mix eggs and milk together and then blend into remaining mixture in bowl.

Spread batter into prepared pan. Sprinkle blackberries evenly over the top. Sprinkle reserved crumb mixture over fruit.

Pour batter into prepared pan. Bake in the preheated oven for 25 to 30 minutes, or until a toothpick inserted into the center of the cake comes out clean.

Easy Stovetop Chicken Teriyaki in Orange Ginger

Ingredients

2 tablespoons canola oil
6 skinless, boneless chicken breast halves
3/4 cup teriyaki sauce
3/4 cup dry white wine
1/2 cup orange marmalade
2 teaspoons minced garlic
1 teaspoon minced fresh ginger root
4 green onions, cut into 1/2-inch pieces

Directions

Heat oil in a large nonstick skillet over medium-high heat, and brown the chicken breasts on both sides, about 6 minutes per side.

Whisk together the teriyaki sauce, white wine, orange marmalade, garlic, ginger, and green onions in a bowl, and pour the sauce over the chicken. Cover the skillet, reduce heat to low, and simmer until chicken is no longer pink in the middle, turning the chicken in the sauce several times as it cooks, 10 to 15 minutes. Serve hot.

Easy Manicotti Florentine

Ingredients

1/2 (10 ounce) package frozen chopped spinach, thawed and drained
1 cup cottage cheese
1/2 cup ricotta cheese
salt to taste
ground black pepper to taste
2 cups tomato sauce
1/4 cup water
1 (8 ounce) package manicotti pasta
1 cup shredded mozzarella cheese

Directions

Preheat oven to 375 degrees F (190 degrees C).

In a large bowl combine spinach, cottage and ricotta cheese. Add salt and pepper to taste. Blend well.

Combine one cup of the spaghetti sauce and the quarter cup of water together. Spread evenly into a 13x9 inch baking dish.

Using a teaspoon, stuff each shell with equal amounts of the cheese mixture. Place stuffed manicotti into baking dish. Pour remaining cup of spaghetti sauce over the top of pasta. Cover with aluminum foil.

Bake in preheated oven for 50 minutes. Uncover and sprinkle with mozzarella cheese. Bake for an additional 10 minutes, or until cheese is melted and bubbly. Let stand 10 to 15 minutes before serving.

Easy Slow Cooker Meatballs

Ingredients

1 1/2 pounds ground beef
1 1/4 cups Italian seasoned bread crumbs
1/4 cup chopped fresh parsley
2 cloves garlic, minced
1 medium yellow onion, chopped
1 egg, beaten
1 (28 ounce) jar spaghetti sauce
1 (16 ounce) can crushed tomatoes
1 (14.25 ounce) can tomato puree

Directions

In a bowl, mix the ground beef, bread crumbs, parsley, garlic, onion, and egg. Shape the mixture into 16 meatballs.

In a slow cooker, mix the spaghetti sauce, crushed tomatoes, and tomato puree. Place the meatballs into the sauce mixture. Cook on Low for 6 to 8 hours.

Easy Swedish Pancakes

Ingredients

- eggs
- cups milk
- /2 cup all-purpose flour
- tablespoon sugar
- pinch salt
- tablespoons melted butter

Directions

In a large bowl, beat eggs with a wire whisk. Mix in milk, flour, sugar, salt, and melted butter.

Preheat a non-stick electric skillet to medium heat. Pour a thin layer of batter on skillet, and spread to edges. Cook until top surface appears dry. Cut into 2 or 4 sections, and flip with a spatula. Cook for another 2 minutes, or until golden brown. Roll each pancake up, and serve.

Easy Vegetable Beef Soup

Ingredients

2 pounds lean ground beef
4 (15 ounce) cans mixed vegetables
4 (16 ounce) cans diced tomatoes
1 onion, chopped
ground black pepper to taste
salt to taste

Directions

In a large soup pot, cook ground meat over medium heat until browned. Drain grease from the pot.

Add chopped onion, mixed vegetables, and tomatoes. Give it a stir. Reduce heat, and simmer for about 3 to 4 hours. Season to taste with salt and pepper.

Easy Valentine Sandwich Cookies

Ingredients

1 cup butter
1 1/2 cups confectioners' sugar 1
egg
1 teaspoon vanilla extract
1/2 teaspoon almond extract
(optional)
2 1/2 cups all-purpose flour
1 teaspoon baking soda
1 teaspoon cream of tartar

Directions

In a large bowl, cream together butter and confectioners' sugar. Beat in egg, vanilla and almond extract. Mix well.

In a medium bowl, stir together flour, baking soda and cream of tartar; blend into the butter mixture. Divide dough into thirds and shape into balls.

Working with 1/3 of dough at a time, roll out dough into desired thickness on a lightly floured surface. For each heart sandwich cookie, cut out 2 3-inch hearts. Cut out the center of ONE of the 3-inch hearts with the 1 1/2-inch cutter.

Place each piece separately on an ungreased cookie sheet, 1 - 2 inches apart. Bake in a preheated, 350 degrees F (175 degrees C) oven until lightly browned (7-8 minutes for 1/4 inch thick cookies). Cool completely on wire rack. Frost bottom cookie with Pink Valentine Frosting and place an open centered cookie on top to form the sandwich. Also frost the small 1 1/2 inch hearts and serve as separate cookies.

Easy Key Lime Pie II

Ingredients

1 (9 inch) prepared graham cracker crust
3 eggs, separated
1 (14 ounce) can sweetened condensed milk
1 teaspoon grated lime zest
1/3 cup fresh lime juice
1 cup frozen whipped topping, thawed (optional)

Directions

Preheat oven to 250 degrees F (125 degrees C).

In a large glass or metal bowl, beat egg whites until stiff peaks form. Set aside.

In a medium bowl, beat egg yolks, then stir in condensed milk, lime rind, and lime juice. Mix well, then fold mixture into beaten egg whites. Pour mixture into graham cracker crust.

Bake in preheated oven for 10 minutes. Chill before serving. Garnish with whipped topping if desired.

Easy-Peezy Caramel Granola

Ingredients

cups quick cooking oats
cup brown sugar
tablespoons ground cinnamon
/2 cup butter, melted
tablespoons caramel sauce
tablespoons white sugar

Directions

Stir together the oats, brown sugar, and cinnamon in a wok or large skillet over high heat, cook 5 to 10 minutes; remove from heat and add the butter and caramel sauce; stir until evenly coated. Spread the mixture onto a flat platter or baking sheet in a thin layer. Sprinkle the white sugar over the granola. Allow to cool completely before serving.

Quick and Easy Spinach Bread

Ingredients

1 tablespoon olive oil
1 clove garlic, minced
1 (10 ounce) package frozen chopped spinach, thawed and drained
1 to taste salt and pepper to taste
1/4 cup grated Parmesan cheese
garlic powder to taste
1 (10 ounce) can refrigerated pizza crust dough
1 cup shredded mozzarella cheese

Directions

Preheat oven to 350 degrees F (175 degrees C). Spray a baking sheet with non-stick cooking spray.

Heat olive oil in a skillet or frying pan over medium heat. Add garlic and saute until soft, about two minutes. Add spinach and cook until liquid has evaporated. Stir in salt, pepper, Parmesan and garlic powder. Remove from heat and let cool.

On a lightly floured surface, roll out pizza crust into a 10x14 inch rectangle. Spread spinach mixture and mozzarella cheese on top of dough. Starting from on end, roll up the crust to make one large loaf. Pinch seam to seal. Place loaf onto prepared baking sheet.

Bake in preheated oven for 20 to 25 minutes, until golden brown.

Easy Vegetarian Corn Chowder

Ingredients

6 tablespoons butter
1/4 cup diced onion
1/2 cup diced celery
6 tablespoons all-purpose flour
2 (14.5 ounce) cans vegetable broth
2 (15 ounce) cans creamed corn
1 (15 ounce) can whole kernel corn, drained
2 tablespoons shredded carrot
1 cup half-and-half cream
3/4 cup skim milk
1/2 teaspoon ground nutmeg
1/4 teaspoon ground black pepper
1 pinch salt

Directions

In a large saucepan over medium heat, melt butter. Cook onions and celery in butter 3 minutes. Whisk in flour and cook 6 minutes more, until light brown. Whisk in broth and simmer 10 minutes.

Stir in creamed corn, corn, carrot, half-and-half, milk, nutmeg, pepper and salt. Simmer over low heat 10 minutes more.

Mom's Easy Creamed Chipped Beef on Toast

Ingredients

5 cups milk
3/4 cup all-purpose flour
1/2 teaspoon salt
1/4 teaspoon ground black pepper
1/2 cup butter
12 ounces beef lunch meat (such as Carl Buddig ®)
16 slices bread, toasted

Directions

Whisk the milk, flour, salt, and pepper together in a bowl until smooth.

Melt the butter in a large pot over medium heat. Gradually stir in the milk mixture until thick. Add the beef; cook and stir until heated through, about 5 minutes. Pour over toast to serve.

Easy Venison Stew

Ingredients

pounds venison stew meat
(10.75 ounce) can condensed
cream of mushroom soup
(10.75 ounce) can condensed
golden mushroom soup
/2 onion, chopped
carrots, cut into 1 inch pieces

Directions

In a slow cooker, combine venison, cream of mushroom soup, golden mushroom soup, onion and carrots. Cover and cook on low setting for 6 to 8 hours.

Easy Pina Colada French Toast

Ingredients

8 eggs
2/3 cup milk
1/2 cup bottled pina colada drink mix
1 tablespoon butter, or as needed
12 (1/2 inch thick) slices French bread
2 bananas, sliced

Directions

Whisk together the eggs, milk, and pina colada mix in a bowl. Heat a skillet over medium heat; melt butter in the skillet until the foam disappears. Soak the bread slices in the egg mixture, turning the slices over a couple of times.

Gently lay the soaked bread slices into the hot skillet 2 at a time and pan-fry until the french toast is golden brown, about 2 minutes per side. Transfer cooked french toast slices to a warmed platter while you finish cooking. Top each 2-slice serving with several slices of banana to serve.

Easy Corn and Green Onion Salad

Ingredients

1 (16 ounce) package frozen corn kernels, thawed
1 green onion, chopped
1 1/2 tablespoons white wine vinegar
1 tablespoon olive oil
1 teaspoon fresh lemon juice
1 1/2 teaspoons dried tarragon leaves
salt and ground black pepper to taste
1 pinch seafood seasoning (such as Old Bay®), or to taste (optional)

Directions

Stir the corn, onion, vinegar, olive oil, lemon juice, tarragon, salt, and pepper together in a bowl. Season with seafood seasoning as desired.

Easy Easy Casserole

Ingredients

1 1/2 pounds ground turkey
4 potatoes, peeled and sliced
2 tablespoons butter
salt and pepper to taste
1 (15 ounce) can cream-style corn
1 (10.75 ounce) can condensed tomato soup

Directions

Preheat oven to 350 degrees F (175 degrees C).

In a large skillet over medium-high heat, place the turkey and saute for 5 to 10 minutes, or until browned.

Place the sliced potatoes in the bottom of a lightly greased 2-quart casserole dish, cover with butter and season with salt and pepper to taste. Then layer the cream-style corn over the potatoes, top with the browned turkey meat, and then top with the tomato soup.

Cover and bake at 350 degrees F (175 degrees C) for 60 minutes.

Easy Shrimp Dinner

Ingredients

2 1/2 cups water
3 cubes chicken bouillon
3 pounds shrimp, peeled and deveined
1/3 cup chopped green onion
1/4 cup soy sauce
salt to taste
1/4 cup cornstarch
1/4 cup cold water
12 ounces trimmed snow peas
4 small ripe tomatoes, diced

Directions

In a large saucepan, heat 2 1/2 cups water to a boil over medium-high heat. Dissolve bouillon in boiling water. Add shrimp, green onion, soy sauce and salt. Boil for 3 minutes.

Dissolve cornstarch in cold water; stir into shrimp mixture. Cook until sauce is thick, then add tomatoes and snow peas. Serve hot.

Easy Portobello Mushroom Saute

Ingredients

3 tablespoons olive oil, divided
1 1/2 tablespoons garlic flavored olive oil
1/4 onion, cut into chunks
2 portobello mushroom caps, sliced
salt and black pepper to taste
freshly grated Parmesan
freshly grated Asiago cheese

Directions

Warm 1 1/2 tablespoons olive oil and 1 1/2 tablespoons garlic flavored olive oil in a skillet over medium heat. Stir in onions and mushrooms; reduce heat to low, and cook until the mushrooms are soft and blackened and the onions are black around the edges. (Add additional olive oil as needed.) Turn the heat off, drizzle with 1 1/2 tablespoons olive oil, and season with salt and pepper. Sprinkle generously with Parmesan and Asiago cheeses.

Quick and Easy Chocolate Chip Bars

Ingredients

1 (18.25 ounce) package yellow
cake mix
1/3 cup brown sugar
1 tablespoon all-purpose flour
1 tablespoon butter, melted
2 tablespoons light corn syrup
1 egg
1 tablespoon water
1/2 teaspoon vanilla extract
1/2 cup semisweet chocolate
chips
1/2 cup chopped walnuts

Directions

Preheat oven to 350 degrees F (175 degrees C). Grease and flour a 9x9 inch pan.

In a large bowl, combine the cake mix, brown sugar and flour. Add the melted butter, corn syrup, egg, water and vanilla; mix until well blended. Stir in the chocolate chips and nuts. Spread batter evenly into the prepared pan.

Bake for 25 to 30 minutes in the preheated oven, until golden brown. Cool, and cut into bars.

Easy Mandarin Orange Cheesecake

Ingredients

CRUST:
1 cup graham cracker crumbs
1/4 cup sugar
1/4 cup butter or margarine, melted
FILLING:
2 (8 ounce) packages cream cheese, softened
1 cup sugar
1/4 cup frozen orange juice concentrate, thawed
2 teaspoons orange extract
1 cup whipping cream, whipped
2 teaspoons grated orange peel
1 (11 ounce) can mandarin orange sections, drained and patted dry

Directions

Combine crust ingredients and press into the bottom of a 9-in. pie plate. Bake at 350 degrees F for 6-8 minute or until lightly browned. Cool. Meanwhile, for filling, beat cream cheese and sugar in a mixing bowl until light and fluffy. Add concentrate and extract; beat well. Fold in whipped cream, and orange peel if desired. Spread evenly into crust. Arrange oranges in decorative design on top of filling. Chill at least 3 hours.

Easy Cheesy Tuna Casserole

Ingredients

(16 ounce) package medium seashell pasta

tablespoon vegetable oil

(10.75 ounce) can condensed cream of mushroom soup

(15 ounce) can mixed vegetables, drained

(6 ounce) can tuna, drained

cups shredded Cheddar cheese

salt and pepper to taste

Directions

Bring a large pot of lightly salted water to a boil. Add 1 tablespoon oil to the water to prevent sticking. Add pasta and cook for 8 to 10 minutes or until al dente; drain. Preheat oven to 350 degrees F (175 degrees C).

In a 2 quart saucepan over medium heat, combine the cream of mushroom soup, mixed vegetables, canned tuna, and 1 cup of the cheddar cheese. Gently fold pasta into the soup mixture and mix thoroughly. Pour pasta and soup mixture into a 11x7 inch baking dish. Sprinkle remaining cup of cheese on top.

Bake in a preheated oven until cheese is melted and bubbly.

Easy Horseradish Dressing

Ingredients

1 cup plain yogurt
1/2 cup sour cream
1/4 cup prepared horseradish
2 tablespoons chopped green onion
1/2 cup mayonnaise
1/2 teaspoon salt
1/2 teaspoon ground black pepper

Directions

In a small bowl, whisk together the yogurt, sour cream, horseradish, green onion, mayonnaise, salt and pepper until well combined. Cover and chill until serving.

Easy Berry "Torte"

Ingredients

15 NABISCO Ginger Snaps, finely crushed
25 NILLA Wafers, finely crushed
1/2 cup PLANTERS Chopped Pecans
1/3 cup butter, melted
1 (8 ounce) package PHILADELPHIA Cream Cheese, softened
1/4 cup sugar
1 teaspoon vanilla
2 cups blueberries
2 cups raspberries

Directions

Heat oven to 375 degrees F. Mix cookie crumbs, nuts and butter; press onto bottom and 1 inch up side of 9-inch springform pan. Bake 5 min.; cool completely.

Beat cream cheese, sugar and vanilla with mixer until blended; spread onto bottom of crust. Top with berries.

Refrigerate 4 hours or until firm.

Krissy's Easy Chocolate Triple Layer Pie

Ingredients

2 cups cold milk
2 (3.9 ounce) packages instant chocolate pudding mix
1 (9 inch) prepared graham cracker crust, chocolate
1 (8 ounce) container frozen whipped topping, thawed
1/2 cup chocolate shavings

Directions

In a large bowl, mix milk and pudding. Beat with wire whisk for 1 minute. Spoon 1 1/2 cups of pudding into graham cracker crust.

Gently fold in 1/2 of the whipped topping into remaining pudding. Spread this mixture over the pudding layer in crust. Top with remaining whipped topping. Garnish with chocolate shavings and cover and refrigerate for 4 hours.

Extra Easy Fudge

Ingredients

2 cups milk chocolate chips
2 1/2 cups prepared chocolate
frosting
1 cup chopped walnuts

Directions

Line one 8x8 inch square pan with foil. Lightly butter the foil.

In a small saucepan melt the chocolate chips over low heat, stirring constantly. Remove the melted chocolate from the heat and stir in the frosting and the nuts stirring until smooth. Pour into the prepared pan and refrigerate until firm. Once firm cut in small squares.

Easy Chicken Curry

Ingredients

6 skinless, boneless chicken breast halves - cut into strips
1/4 cup olive oil
2 large onions, diced
1/3 cup curry powder, or to taste

Directions

Heat oil in a large skillet over medium heat. Add onion and saute until soft and golden brown. Slowly stir in curry powder. Once ingredients are blended together, add chicken breasts. Cover skillet and simmer over medium low heat for about 45 minutes or until chicken is cooked through and no longer pink inside.

Remove cover from skillet and cook for an additional 15 minutes, until sauce reduces. (Note: Make sure that you stir and that dish does not burn, as curry powder burns very easily!)

Easy Butter Chicken

Ingredients

4 boneless skinless chicken breast halves
salt and pepper to taste
1 teaspoon dried tarragon
1 tablespoon fresh lemon juice
1/4 cup butter

Directions

Preheat the oven to 400 degrees F (200 degrees C).

Season the chicken with salt, pepper and tarragon; drizzle with lemon juice. Set aside.

Place an oven proof skillet or Dutch oven over medium heat and melt the butter. Place the chicken in the dish, turning to coat both sides. Cover the chicken with a sheet of parchment paper, and then cover with a lid.

Bake in the preheated oven for 10 to 15 minutes, or until chicken is cooked through.

Easy Marinated Mushrooms

Ingredients

2 cups soy sauce
2 cups water
1 cup butter
2 cups white sugar
4 (8 ounce) packages fresh mushrooms, stems removed

Directions

In a medium saucepan over low heat, mix soy sauce, water and butter. Stir until the butter has melted, then gradually mix in the sugar until it is completely dissolved.

Place mushrooms in a slow cooker set to low, and cover with the soy sauce mixture. Cook 8 to 10 hours, stirring approximately every hour. Chill in the refrigerator until serving.

Easy Surprise Cake

ngredients

3 tablespoons butter, softened
 cup white sugar
 eggs
 3/4 cups all-purpose flour
 1/2 teaspoons baking powder

Directions

Preheat an oven to 350 degrees F (175 degrees C). Grease 2 8-inch cake pans.

Place the butter and sugar into a mixing bowl, and mash together with a wooden spoon until the mixture is creamy and thoroughly combined. In a separate bowl, beat the eggs, and pour into the butter mixture. Stir until combined.

Sift the flour and baking powder together in a bowl, and lightly stir into the butter mixture. Pour half the batter into each prepared cake pan.

Bake in the preheated oven until a toothpick inserted into the middle of a cake comes out clean, 20 to 25 minutes. Cool in pans for 10 minutes before removing to finish cooling on wire racks.

Easy Tilapia with Wine and Tomatoes

Ingredients

4 (4 ounce) fillets tilapia
salt and pepper to taste
4 tablespoons butter
3 cloves garlic, pressed
4 fresh basil leaves, chopped
1 large tomato, chopped
1 cup white wine

Directions

Preheat a grill for medium-high heat.

Place the tilapia fillets side by side on a large piece of aluminum foil. Season each one with salt and pepper. Place one tablespoon of butter on top of each piece of fish, and sprinkle garlic, basil and tomato. Pour the wine over everything. Fold foil up around fish, and seal into a packet. Place packet on a cookie sheet for ease in transportation to and from the grill.

Place foil packet on the preheated grill, and cook for 15 minutes, or until fish flakes easily with a fork. Open the packet carefully so as not to get burned from the steam, and serve.

Easy Arugula Salad

Ingredients

4 cups young arugula leaves, rinsed and dried
1 cup cherry tomatoes, halved
1/4 cup pine nuts
2 tablespoons grapeseed oil or olive oil
1 tablespoon rice vinegar
salt to taste
freshly ground black pepper to taste
1/4 cup grated Parmesan cheese
1 large avocado - peeled, pitted and sliced

Directions

In a large plastic bowl with a lid, combine arugula, cherry tomatoes, pine nuts, oil, vinegar, and Parmesan cheese. Season with salt and pepper to taste. Cover, and shake to mix.

Divide salad onto plates, and top with slices of avocado.

Amazingly Easy Irish Soda Bread

Ingredients

4 cups all-purpose flour
4 tablespoons white sugar
1 teaspoon baking soda
1 tablespoon baking powder
1/2 teaspoon salt
1/2 cup margarine, softened
1 cup buttermilk
1 egg
1/4 cup butter, melted
1/4 cup buttermilk

Directions

Preheat oven to 375 degrees F (190 degrees C). Lightly grease a large baking sheet.

In a large bowl, mix together flour, sugar, baking soda, baking powder, salt and margarine. Stir in 1 cup of buttermilk and egg. Turn dough out onto a lightly floured surface and knead slightly. Form dough into a round and place on prepared baking sheet. In a small bowl, combine melted butter with 1/4 cup buttermilk; brush loaf with this mixture. Use a sharp knife to cut an 'X' into the top of the loaf.

Bake in preheated oven for 45 to 50 minutes, or until a toothpick inserted into the center of the loaf comes out clean, about 30 to 50 minutes. You may continue to brush the loaf with the butter mixture while it bakes.

Easy Cheesy Skillet Chicken

Ingredients

skinless, boneless chicken breast halves

(10.75 ounce) can condensed cream of mushroom soup

(12 fluid ounce) can evaporated milk

slices American processed cheese, cut into 1-inch pieces

Directions

In a large skillet, brown chicken on both sides. In the meantime, in a medium bowl combine the soup, milk and cheese. Mix together. When chicken is browned, pour mixture over chicken pieces. Cook over medium low heat until chicken is done and juices run clear. Serve.

Herald's Impossibly Easy Cheeseburger Pie

Ingredients

1 pound ground beef
1 onion, chopped
2 cloves garlic, minced
1 tomato, sliced
1/2 teaspoon garlic salt
1 teaspoon ground black pepper
1 teaspoon dried oregano
1 cup shredded Cheddar cheese
1/2 cup buttermilk baking mix
1 cup milk
2 eggs

Directions

Preheat oven to 400 degrees F (200 degrees C). Grease a 10 inch deep dish pie plate.

Heat a large skillet over medium heat. Add ground beef, onion, and garlic; cook and stir until beef is brown. Drain off fat. Spread into prepared pie plate.

Sprinkle meat with salt, black pepper, and oregano. Arrange tomato slices over meat, spread shredded cheese on top.

In a small bowl, mix together baking mix, milk and eggs. Pour over cheese.

Bake for about 25 minutes, or until knife inserted in center comes out clean. Cool for 5 minutes before serving.

Really Easy Chowder

Ingredients

1 (14.5 ounce) can diced tomatoes
3 stalks celery, chopped
1 teaspoon dried oregano
1 teaspoon dried basil
salt and pepper to taste
1/2 pound frozen cod fillets

Directions

In a medium sized stock pot place undrained tomatoes, celery, oregano, basil, salt and pepper. Bring to a boil over medium heat.

Place frozen fish filets in pot. Reduce heat and cook for 10 to 15 minutes. Cook until mixture is heated through and fish is opaque and flaky. Thin with a little water if desired.

Easy Smoked Salmon Pasta

Ingredients

1 (8 ounce) package linguine pasta
1 tablespoon butter
1 tablespoon extra-virgin olive oil
1 shallot, minced
1 ounce smoked salmon, cut into small pieces
1 tablespoon reduced-fat cream cheese
3 tablespoons milk

Directions

Fill a large pot with lightly-salted water and bring to a rolling boil. Stir the linguine into the water and return to a boil. Cook uncovered until the pasta has cooked through but is still firm to the bite, about 11 minutes; drain, reserving 2 tablespoons of the water.

Melt the butter with the olive oil in a saucepan over medium-low heat; when the mixture begins to bubble, add the shallots and cook until softened. Stir the salmon, cream cheese, and milk into the shallot mixture. Mix the reserved water from the pasta into the mixture. Transfer to a large bowl and toss with the pasta to serve.

Easy Chickpea Curry

Ingredients

tablespoon butter
onion, chopped
cloves garlic, minced
teaspoons curry powder
teaspoons garam masala
/2 teaspoon ground paprika
/2 teaspoon white sugar
/2 teaspoon ground ginger
/4 teaspoon ground turmeric
/4 teaspoon salt
/4 teaspoon pepper
(15 ounce) can garbanzo beans,
drained
potatoes, chopped
(14 ounce) can coconut milk
tomato, chopped
/3 cup milk
tablespoons ketchup
tablespoons sour cream
cubes chicken bouillon
/4 cup ground almonds, or as
needed

Directions

Melt the butter over medium heat in a large saucepan. Cook and stir the onion and garlic in the melted butter for about 5 minutes, until onion is translucent. Sprinkle in curry powder, garam masala, paprika, sugar, ginger, turmeric, salt, and pepper. Continue to cook and stir 3 to 4 more minutes, until spices are lightly toasted.

Mix in the garbanzo beans, potatoes, coconut milk, tomato, milk, ketchup, sour cream, and bouillon cubes. Simmer the curry over medium-low heat for about 25 minutes, until the potatoes are tender. Stir in ground almonds to thicken.

Very Easy Risotto

Ingredients

2 tablespoons butter
2/3 cup sliced green onion
1 1/3 cups uncooked long-grain rice
4 cups water
1 teaspoon chicken bouillon granules
1/4 teaspoon ground black pepper
3/4 cup grated Parmesan cheese

Directions

Melt butter in a large skillet over medium-high heat. Cook green onions in butter briefly, then add the rice. Cook and stir for a few minutes to toast rice. Stir in water, and season with chicken bouillon and pepper. Bring to a boil, then reduce heat to medium-low. Cover, and simmer for 20 minutes.

Remove from heat, cover, and let stand for 5 minutes. Stir in the Parmesan cheese.

Quick and Easy Taco Dip

Ingredients

1 (8 ounce) package cream cheese, softened
3/4 teaspoon taco seasoning mix
1/3 cup salsa
1 (8 ounce) package shredded Cheddar cheese

Directions

In a medium bowl, mix the cream cheese, taco seasoning mix and salsa. Spread the mixture into a shallow serving dish or an 8 inch baking pan. Top with Cheddar cheese. Chill in the refrigerator approximately 1 hour before serving.

Quick and Super Easy Chicken and Dumplings

Ingredients

2 1/4 cups biscuit baking mix
2/3 cup milk
2 (14 ounce) cans chicken broth
2 (10 ounce) cans chunk chicken, drained

Directions

In a medium bowl, stir together the biscuit mix and milk just until it pulls together. Set aside.

Pour the cans of chicken broth into a saucepan along with the chicken; bring to a boil. Once the broth is at a steady boil, take a handful of biscuit dough and flatten it in your hand. Tear off 1 to 2 inch pieces and drop them into the boiling broth. Make sure they are fully immersed at least for a moment. Once all of the dough is in the pot, carefully stir so that the newest dough clumps get covered by the broth. Cover, and simmer over medium heat for about 10 minutes, stirring occasionally.

Easy French Toast

Ingredients

egg
3/4 cup milk
tablespoon ground cinnamon
teaspoon vanilla extract
pinch salt
slices bread

Directions

Beat together egg, milk, cinnamon, vanilla and salt.

Heat a lightly oiled skillet or griddle over medium heat.

Soak bread slices in egg mixture for 20 second on each side, or until thoroughly coated. Cook bread until both sides are lightly browned and crisp. Serve hot.

Easy Tilapia

Ingredients

2 (3 ounce) fillets tilapia fillets
2 tablespoons olive oil
salt and pepper to taste
1 lemon, halved
1/2 cup white wine
2 tomatoes, seeded and chopped
3 tablespoons capers
1 cup asparagus spears, trimmed and cut in half
3 tablespoons butter

Directions

Heat a large non-stick skillet over medium heat. Drizzle fillets with olive oil and season with salt and pepper. Place fillets in skillet and sprinkle with half of the lemon over. Cook for 3 minutes per side, or until fish flakes easily with a fork. Transfer fillets to a plate, and keep warm.

Add wine, remaining 1/2 lemon, tomatoes, capers, and salt and pepper to the skillet. Increase heat to medium high and boil for 2 minutes to burn off alcohol. Reduce heat to low and return fillets to the pan along with the asparagus. Cover and simmer 2 minutes more, then transfer fish and asparagus to a serving dish and keep warm.

Again, increase heat to medium high and whisk in butter, and boil to desired consistency. Spoon sauce over fish, and serve.

Super Easy Mardi Gras King Cake

Ingredients

3 (14 ounce) cans refrigerated
sweet roll dough
2 (12 fluid ounce) cans creamy
vanilla ready-to-spread frosting
1/4 cup milk
2 drops green food coloring
2 drops yellow food coloring
1 drop red food coloring
1 drop blue food coloring
1/2 cup multi-colored sprinkles

Directions

Preheat oven to 350 degrees F (175 degrees C). Grease a baking sheet.

Open the cans of sweet roll dough and unroll the dough from each can into 3 strands. Working on a clean surface, place 3 dough strands side by side and gather them together to make one large strand. Fold this in half, and roll slightly to make a fat log. Repeat steps with the remaining dough. Place each log on the prepared baking sheet and shape to make a ring, overlapping the ends and pinching them together to make a complete circle. Pat the dough into shape as necessary to make the ring even in size all the way around. Cover loosely with foil.

Bake in preheated oven until firm to the touch and golden brown, 50 to 60 minutes. Check often for doneness so the ring doesn't overbake. Place on a wire rack and cool completely.

Place the cake ring on a serving plate. Cut a slit along the inside of the ring and insert a small plastic baby, pushing it far enough into the cake to be hidden from view.

Divide the frosting evenly between 4 bowls. Stir 1 tablespoon of milk into each bowl to thin the frosting. Use the frosting in one bowl to drizzle over the cooled cake. To the remaining three bowls of frosting, stir yellow food coloring into one and green into another. Stir the red and blue food colorings together with the frosting in a third bowl to make purple frosting. Drizzle the cake with yellow, green, and purple frostings in any desired pattern. Dust the cake with multi-colored sprinkles and decorate with beads, additional plastic babies, curly ribbon, and other festive trinkets.

Easy Eggnog Ice Cream

Ingredients

2 cups eggnog
1 cup heavy whipping cream
1 cup milk

Directions

Mix the eggnog, whipping cream, and milk together in a bowl, and pour the mixture into the freezer container of an ice cream maker. Freeze according to manufacturer's directions. Once frozen, spoon the ice cream into a container, and freeze 2 hours more.

Easy Pavlova

ngredients

- egg whites
- 1/4 cups white sugar
- teaspoon vanilla extract
- teaspoon lemon juice
- teaspoons cornstarch
- pint heavy cream
- kiwi, peeled and sliced

Directions

Pre-heat oven to 300 degrees F (150 degrees C). Line a baking sheet with parchment paper. Draw a 9 inch circle on the parchment paper.

In a large bowl, beat egg whites until stiff but not dry. Gradually add in the sugar, 1 tablespoon at a time, beating well after each addition. Beat until thick and glossy. Overbeaten egg whites lose volume and deflate when folded into other ingredients. Be absolutely sure not a particle of grease or egg yolk gets into the whites. Gently fold in vanilla extract, lemon juice and cornstarch.

Spoon mixture inside the circle drawn on the parchment paper. Working from the center, spread mixture toward the outside edge, building edge slightly. This should leave a slight depression in the center.

Bake for 1 hour. Cool on a wire rack.

Remove the paper, and place meringue on a flat serving plate. Fill the center of the meringue with whipped cream, sweetened if desired. Top whipped cream with kiwifruit slices.

Easy Lemon Lush

Ingredients

2 cups all-purpose flour
1 cup butter, softened
2 (8 ounce) packages cream cheese
1 cup SPLENDA® No Calorie Sweetener, Granulated
2 (3.4 ounce) packages instant lemon pudding mix
3 1/2 cups milk
1 (12 ounce) container frozen whipped topping, thawed

Directions

Preheat oven to 350 degrees F (175 degrees C). In a medium bowl, combine the flour and butter using a pastry cutter until a ball forms. Press into the bottom of a 9x13 inch baking dish.

Bake for 25 minutes in the preheated oven, or until lightly golden. Remove from oven and allow to cool completely.

In a medium bowl, beat the cream cheese and SPLENDA® Granulated Sweetener together until smooth and well blended. Spread evenly over the cooled crust. In another bowl, whisk together the lemon pudding mix and milk for 3 to 5 minutes. Spread over the cream cheese layer. Chill until set, then top with whipped topping.

Easy Pumpkin Rice

Ingredients

4 cups instant rice
4 cups water
1 (29 ounce) can pumpkin puree
1 1/2 teaspoons pumpkin pie spice
1 1/2 cups brown sugar
1/2 cup butter
salt to taste

Directions

Combine the rice and water in a large saucepan over medium heat; bring to a boil; cover and reduce heat to medium-low; simmer until the water is completely absorbed, 15 to 20 minutes.

Stir together the pumpkin puree, pumpkin pie spice, brown sugar, butter, and salt in a separate saucepan over medium-low heat. Cook until warm. Stir pumpkin mixture into cooked rice.

Easy Avocado Spread

Ingredients

2 ripe avocados - peeled, pitted, and mashed
1 (1 ounce) package ranch dressing mix
2 tablespoons fresh lemon juice
1 tablespoon light mayonnaise

Directions

Stir together the avocados, ranch dressing mix, lemon juice, and light mayonnaise. Chill for 1 hour.

Easy Peach Cobbler

Ingredients

cup white sugar
/2 cup butter, room temperature
cup self-rising flour
cup milk
(15 ounce) can peaches

Directions

Preheat oven to 350 degrees F (175 degrees C).

In a one-quart baking dish or 9 inch square pan, cream together sugar and butter. Mix in flour and milk until smooth. Pour peaches and their juice over the top.

Bake 25 to 30 minutes in the preheated oven, until golden brown.

Easy Pumpkin Turnovers

Ingredients

1 cup canned pumpkin
1/4 cup brown sugar
2 teaspoons ground cinnamon
2 teaspoons pumpkin pie spice
2 sheets frozen puff pastry, thawed

Directions

Preheat an oven to 350 degrees F (175 degrees C). Line two baking sheets with parchment paper.

Mix pumpkin, brown sugar, cinnamon, and pumpkin pie spice in a bowl.

Roll out puff pastry into a 12x12 inch square and cut each sheet into 9 - 4 inch squares.

Spoon pumpkin mix into center of pastry squares; wet edges of each square with water, fold over, corner to corner, and pinch edges together. Place onto prepared baking sheets.

Bake in the preheated oven until pastry is puffed and golden brown, about 15 minutes. Cool on the pans for 10 minutes. Remove to a wire rack and cool completely.

Easy Asian Quiche

Ingredients

3 eggs, beaten
2 cups bean sprouts
2 cups Swiss cheese
1/2 cup biscuit baking mix (such as Bisquick®)
1 tablespoon garlic powder
1/3 cup chopped onion
1/2 cup chopped green onion
1 cup Kikkoman PEARL Original Soymilk
2 teaspoons ginger powder
1 (9 inch) uncooked pie crust

Directions

Line a 9-inch pie plate with the uncooked crust.

Combine all ingredients in a large bowl, mixing well. Pour into the prepared pie plate and bake at 375 degrees for 45 minutes.

Easy Lemon Bars for Junior Chefs

Ingredients

1 (16 ounce) package angel food cake mix
1 (21 ounce) can lemon pie filling

Directions

Preheat oven to 350 degrees F (175 degrees C).

Combine the angel food cake mix with the lemon pie filling in a mixing bowl; blend until smooth. Pour the batter into an ungreased 10x15 inch jelly roll pan.

Bake in preheated oven until golden brown and top springs back when lightly touched, 20 to 25 minutes. Cool in the pan, and cut into squares.

Best Toffee Ever - Super Easy

Ingredients

cups butter

cups white sugar

/4 teaspoon salt

cups semisweet chocolate chips

cup finely chopped almonds

Directions

In a large heavy bottomed saucepan, combine the butter, sugar and salt. Cook over medium heat, stirring until the butter is melted. Allow to come to a boil, and cook until the mixture becomes a dark amber color, and the temperature has reached 285 degrees F (137 degrees C). Stir occasionally.

While the toffee is cooking, cover a large baking sheet with aluminum foil or parchment paper.

As soon as the toffee reaches the proper temperature, pour it out onto the prepared baking sheet. Sprinkle the chocolate over the top, and let it set for a minute or two to soften. Spread the chocolate into a thin even layer once it is melted. Sprinkle the nuts over the chocolate, and press in slightly. Putting a plastic bag over your hand will minimize the mess.

Place the toffee in the refrigerator to chill until set. Break into pieces, and store in an airtight container.

Easy Sour Cream Raisin Pie

Ingredients

1 (9 inch) unbaked pie crust
2 eggs
1 cup sour cream
3/4 cup white sugar
1 teaspoon vanilla extract
1/4 teaspoon salt
1/4 teaspoon ground nutmeg
1 cup raisins

Directions

Preheat oven to 375 degrees F (190 degrees C.)

In a large bowl, combine eggs, sour cream, sugar, vanilla, salt and nutmeg. Beat until smooth. stir in raisins. Pour filling into pie crust.

Bake in the lower half of preheated oven for 40 minutes, or until filling is set. Allow to cool before serving.

Very Easy Mushroom Barley Soup

Ingredients

1/4 cup olive oil
1 cup chopped onion
3/4 cup diced carrots
1/2 cup chopped celery
1 teaspoon minced garlic
1 pound sliced fresh mushrooms
6 cups chicken broth
3/4 cup barley
salt and pepper to taste

Directions

Heat the oil in a large soup pot over medium heat. Add the onion, carrots, celery and garlic; cook and stir until onions are tender and transparent. Stir in mushrooms and continue to cook for a few minutes. Pour in the chicken broth and add barley. Bring to a boil, then reduce heat to low. Cover and simmer until barley is tender, about 50 minutes. Season with salt and pepper before serving.

Embarrassingly Easy Barbecue Chicken

Ingredients

1 (3 pound) whole chicken, cut into pieces
1 (12 fluid ounce) can cola-flavored carbonated beverage
14 ounces ketchup

Directions

Preheat oven to 350 degrees F (175 degrees C).

Mix the cola and ketchup in a 9x13 inch baking dish. Add the chicken pieces, turning to coat well. Bake skin side down for 30 minutes. Turn and bake for an additional 30 minutes. Let cool for 10 minutes and serve!

Easy Pasta Fagioli

Ingredients

tablespoon olive oil
carrot, diced
stalk celery, diced
thin slice onion, diced
/2 teaspoon chopped garlic
(8 ounce) cans tomato sauce
(14 ounce) can chicken broth
reshly ground black pepper to
aste
tablespoon dried parsley
/2 tablespoon dried basil leaves
(15 ounce) can cannellini beans,
rained and rinsed
1/2 cups ditalini pasta

Directions

Heat olive oil in a saucepan over medium heat. Saute carrot, celery and onion until soft. Add garlic and saute briefly. Stir in tomato sauce, chicken broth, pepper, parsley and basil; simmer for 20 minutes.

Bring a large pot of lightly salted water to a boil. Add ditalini pasta and cook for 8 minutes or until al dente; drain.

Add beans to the sauce mixture and simmer for a few minutes. When pasta is done, stir into sauce and bean mixture.

Super Easy Hazelnut Pastries

Ingredients

1 (17.25 ounce) package frozen puff pastry, thawed
11 tablespoons chocolate hazelnut spread
1/2 cup chopped hazelnuts (optional)
6 teaspoons powdered sugar

Directions

Preheat oven to 425 degrees F (220 degrees C). Lightly grease a baking sheet.

Unfold the puff pastry on a lightly floured surface, and roll out to a rectangle of about 20x9 inches. Spread the chocolate hazelnut spread over the pastry, then scatter hazelnuts over the top.

Roll the long sides of the pastry rectangle toward the center; where they meet in the center, dampen with water to secure. Using a sharp knife, cut into about 1/2-inch slices; place in the baking sheet, and sprinkle with powdered sugar.

Bake in preheated oven until golden brown, about 10 to 15 minutes.

Easy Caramelized Onion Pork Chops

Ingredients

1 tablespoon vegetable oil
4 (4 ounce) pork loin chops, 1/2 inch thick
3 teaspoons seasoning salt
2 teaspoons ground black pepper
1 onion, cut into strips
1 cup water

Directions

Rub chops with 2 teaspoons seasoning salt and 1 teaspoon pepper, or to taste.

In a skillet, heat oil over medium heat. Brown pork chops on each side. Add the onions and water to the pan. Cover, reduce heat, and simmer for 20 minutes.

Turn chops over, and add remaining salt and pepper. Cover, and cook until water evaporates and onions turn light to medium brown. Remove chops from pan, and serve with onions on top.

Insanely Easy Vegetarian Chili

Ingredients

1 tablespoon vegetable oil
1 cup chopped onions
3/4 cup chopped carrots
3 cloves garlic, minced
1 cup chopped green bell pepper
1 cup chopped red bell pepper
3/4 cup chopped celery
1 tablespoon chili powder
1 1/2 cups chopped fresh mushrooms
1 (28 ounce) can whole peeled tomatoes with liquid, chopped
1 (19 ounce) can kidney beans with liquid
1 (11 ounce) can whole kernel corn, undrained
1 tablespoon ground cumin
1 1/2 teaspoons dried oregano
1 1/2 teaspoons dried basil

Directions

Heat oil in a large saucepan over medium heat. Saute onions, carrots, and garlic until tender. Stir in green pepper, red pepper, celery, and chili powder. Cook until vegetables are tender, about 6 minutes.

Stir in mushrooms, and cook 4 minutes. Stir in tomatoes, kidney beans, and corn. Season with cumin, oregano, and basil. Bring to a boil, and reduce heat to medium. Cover, and simmer for 20 minutes, stirring occasionally.

Easy Slow Cooker Chicken Wings

Ingredients

5 1/2 pounds chicken wings, split and tips discarded

1 (12 fluid ounce) can or bottle chile sauce

1/4 cup fresh lemon juice

1/4 cup molasses

2 tablespoons Worcestershire sauce

3 drops hot pepper sauce

1 tablespoon salsa

2 1/2 teaspoons chili powder

1 teaspoon garlic powder

2 teaspoons salt

Directions

Place chicken in slow cooker. In a medium bowl combine the chile sauce, lemon juice, molasses, Worcestershire sauce, hot pepper sauce, salsa, chili powder, garlic powder and salt. Mix together and pour mixture over chicken.

Cook in slow cooker on Medium Low setting for 5 hours.

Easy Passion Fruit Mousse

Ingredients

1 cup whipping cream
1 cup sweetened condensed milk
1/2 cup frozen passion fruit juice
concentrate

Directions

Pour the whipping cream, condensed milk, and passion fruit juice into a blender. Blend on low until light and fluffy, 30 seconds to 1 minute. Pour into a serving bowl or dessert dishes, and refrigerate at least 30 minutes before serving.

Easy Refrigerator Pickles

Ingredients

5 cups thinly sliced cucumber
2 cups thinly sliced onions
1 1/2 cups sugar
1 1/2 cups cider vinegar
1/2 teaspoon salt
1/2 teaspoon mustard seed
1/2 teaspoon celery seed
1/2 teaspoon ground turmeric
1/2 teaspoon ground cloves

Directions

Place cucumbers and onions in a large bowl; set aside. Combine remaining ingredients in a saucepan; bring to a boil. Cook and stir just until the sugar is dissolved. Pour over cucumber mixture; cool. Cover tightly and refrigerate for at least 24 hours before serving.

Easy Mexican Chicken Bake

Ingredients

6 boneless, chicken breast halves - cooked, skinned
1 (10.75 ounce) can condensed cream of mushroom soup
1 (10.75 ounce) can condensed cream of chicken soup
1 (10.75 ounce) can condensed nacho cheese soup
1 pound processed cheese, cubed
1/2 teaspoon chili powder
1 (14.5 ounce) package nacho-flavor tortilla chips

Directions

Preheat oven to 350 degrees F (175 degrees C).

In a large bowl, combine the chicken, mushroom soup, chicken soup, nacho cheese soup, process cheese food and chili powder to taste.

Spread a layer of tortilla chips in the bottom of a 9x13 inch baking dish. Spread the mixture over the chips and top with the remaining chips.

Bake at 350 degrees F (175 degrees C) for 30 to 45 minutes, or until all the cheese is melted and bubbly.

Lynn's Easy Noodle Pudding

Ingredients

- 1 (16 ounce) package egg noodles
- 2 cups sour cream
- 2 cups creamy whipped cottage cheese
- 1 cup white sugar, divided
- 2 eggs, beaten
- 1 cup raisins
- 1/2 cup butter
- 1 teaspoon ground cinnamon

Directions

Bring a large pot of lightly salted water to a boil. Stir in egg noodles and cook until al dente, 10 to 12 minutes. Drain.

Preheat oven to 350 degrees F (175 degrees C). Lightly grease 13x9 inch baking dish.

Toss the cooked noodles with the sour cream, cottage cheese, 1/2 cup sugar, eggs, and raisins until well blended. Pour the noodle mixture into the prepared pan. Dot the top with small pieces of butter.

Mix the remaining 1/2 cup sugar with the cinnamon. Sprinkle over the noodles.

Bake in preheated oven until top is lightly brown, about 45 minutes. Remove from oven and cool 10 minutes to set pudding before serving.

Easy Seafood Alfredo

Ingredients

16 ounces uncooked black squid ink pasta
1 tablespoon butter
3 cloves garlic, minced
1/2 cup chicken broth
1 cup fat-free half-and-half
6 tablespoons grated Parmesan cheese
1 slice fat-free American cheese, torn into pieces
1 teaspoon dried basil
1 teaspoon dried parsley
ground black pepper to taste
2 (8 ounce) packages imitation crabmeat, flaked

Directions

Bring a large pot of lightly salted water to a boil. Add pasta, cook for 8 to 10 minutes, until al dente, and drain.

Melt the butter in a skillet over medium heat, and cook the garlic 1 minute. Pour in the chicken broth and half-and-half. Cook and stir until heated through.

Mix the Parmesan cheese and American cheese into the skillet. Cook and stir until American cheese is melted. Season the mixture with basil, parsley, and pepper. Mix in the imitation crabmeat, and continue cooking until heated through. Serve over the cooked pasta.

Easy Pumpkin Cream Trifle

Ingredients

1 (18.25 ounce) package spice cake mix
1 (3.4 ounce) package instant vanilla pudding
1 cup pumpkin puree
1/2 cup water
1/2 cup vegetable oil
3 eggs
2 teaspoons pumpkin pie spice
2 cups cold milk
2 (3.4 ounce) packages cheesecake flavor instant pudding and pie filling
2 cups whipped topping
1 cup chopped toasted pecans
1 cup English toffee bits

Directions

Preheat oven to 350 degrees F (175 degrees C). Lightly grease a 9x13 baking dish.

Combine the cake mix, vanilla pudding mix, pumpkin, water, oil, eggs, and pie spice in a large mixing bowl; pour into the prepared dish.

Bake in the preheated oven for 45 to 50 minutes. Allow to cool to room temperature on a wire rack. Cut the cake into 1-inch cubes.

Whisk together the milk and cheesecake pudding mix. Allow to set, about 2 minutes. Fold the whipped topping into the pudding mixture.

Layer 1/3 of the cake cubes into the bottom of a large bowl; top with 1/3 of the cream mixture and sprinkle with 1/3 of the pecans and toffee bit. Repeat layering until all ingredients are uses. Refrigerate 1 hour before serving.

Easy Creamy Chicken Mushroom Sauce

Ingredients

1 tablespoon butter
1 onion, chopped
1 pound fresh mushrooms, sliced
5 cloves garlic, minced
1 pound small shell pasta
1 (10.75 ounce) can condensed cream of mushroom soup
1/8 cup heavy cream
5 teaspoons ground black pepper, or to taste
2 tablespoons paprika
1 pinch salt
3 cups shredded Medium Cheddar cheese
2 cups chicken breasts, cooked and chopped

Directions

In a large skillet, melt butter over medium heat and add onion, mushrooms and garlic; saute until golden brown.

Bring a large pot of lightly salted water to a boil; add pasta and cook for 8 to 10 minutes or until al dente; drain.

In a large saucepan over medium-low heat, combine soup, cream, ground black pepper, paprika and salt; heat until sauce thickens.

Add mushroom mixture to sauce and bring to a slow boil over medium heat; stir in cheese and chopped chicken.

Pour sauce onto pasta; serve.

Easy Honey Mustard Mozzarella Chicken

Ingredients

4 skinless, boneless chicken breast halves
3/4 cup honey
1/2 cup prepared mustard
lemon pepper to taste
4 slices bacon, cut in half
1 cup shredded mozzarella cheese

Directions

Preheat oven to 375 degrees F (190 degrees C).

Place the chicken breast halves in a baking dish, and drizzle evenly with honey and mustard. Sprinkle with lemon pepper.

Bake chicken 25 minutes in the preheated oven. Top each breast half with 2 bacon slice halves, and sprinkle evenly with cheese. Continue baking 10 minutes, or until chicken juices run clear, bacon is crisp, and cheese is bubbly.

Easy Lemon-Pepper Blackened Salmon

Ingredients

2 tablespoons butter, melted
2 tablespoons fresh lemon juice
1 teaspoon chopped fresh parsley
1/2 teaspoon garlic powder
salt and ground black pepper to taste
1 tablespoon whole black peppercorns
4 salmon fillets
2 tablespoons olive oil

Directions

Preheat oven to 350 degrees F (175 degrees C).

Whisk together the butter, lemon juice, parsley, garlic powder, salt, and pepper. Stir in the peppercorns. Dip the salmon into the sauce so the flesh side is coated, and set on a plate,

Heat the olive oil in an ovenproof skillet over medium-high heat. When the oil begins to smoke, add the salmon, placing it skin side up into the skillet. Cook for until the flesh is seared and golden brown, about 1 minute.

Place the skillet into the preheated oven, and cook until the salmon flakes easily with a fork, 10 to 12 minutes. Serve immediately.

Easy Vanilla Cookie

Ingredients

1 (18.25 ounce) package yellow
cake mix
1 egg
1 (8 ounce) container frozen
whipped topping, thawed
2 teaspoons ground cinnamon
2 tablespoons white sugar

Directions

Preheat oven to 350 degrees F (175 degrees C).

In a medium bowl, stir together the cake mix, egg and whipped topping until a dough forms. In a small bowl, stir together the cinnamon and sugar. Roll the dough into walnut sized balls and roll the balls in the cinnamon sugar mixture. Place on an unprepared cookie sheet about 1 to 2 inches apart.

Bake for 12 to 15 minutes in the preheated oven. Cookies will be golden brown. Allow cookies to cool on the baking sheets for a few minutes before removing to cool on wire racks.

Easy Orange Rolls

Ingredients

1 cup sugar
1/2 cup butter or margarine
1/4 cup orange juice
2 tablespoons grated orange peel
3 (10 ounce) cans refrigerated biscuits

Directions

In a saucepan, combine sugar, butter, orange juice and peel. Heat until sugar is dissolved and butter is melted. Pour into a greased 10-in. fluted tube pan. Place 12 biscuits on their sides in a ring around the outer edge, overlapping slightly. Arrange remaining biscuits in the same manner, creating two more rings (one of 10 biscuits and one of eight). Bake at 350 degrees F for 25-30 minutes or until golden brown. Immediately turn upside down onto serving platter. Serve warm.

Easy North Carolina Barbeque

Ingredients

(5 pound) pork butt roast
2 cups white vinegar
cup butter, melted
2 tablespoons salt
2 tablespoons lemon juice
2 tablespoons crushed red pepper
flakes
1 tablespoon hot sauce
1 tablespoon ground black pepper
2 tablespoons white sugar

Directions

Trim the fat from the roast; place in slow cooker and cook on Low overnight, at least 8 hours.

To make the sauce, whisk together the vinegar, melted butter, salt, lemon juice, crushed red pepper, hot sauce, black pepper, and sugar in a bowl.

Carefully remove the roast to a cutting board. Pull the meat from the bone with a fork. Return the pork to the slow cooker. Pour the sauce over the pulled pork. Simmer for 1 hour more.

Easy Chicken Enchiladas

Ingredients

3 cups shredded Cheddar cheese, divided
2 cups shredded Monterey Jack cheese
2 cups chopped cooked chicken
2 cups sour cream
1 (10.75 ounce) can condensed cream of chicken soup, undiluted
1 (4 ounce) can chopped green chilies
2 tablespoons finely chopped onion
1/4 teaspoon pepper
1/8 teaspoon salt
10 (8 inch) flour tortillas, warmed

Directions

In a large bowl, combine 2 cups cheddar cheese, Monterey Jack cheese, chicken, sour cream, soup, chilies, onion, pepper and salt. Spoon about 1/2 cup off center on each tortilla; roll up. Place seam side down in a greased 13-in. x 9-in. x 2-in. baking dish.

Cover and bake at 350 degrees F for 20 minutes. Uncover; sprinkle with remaining cheddar cheese. Bake 5 minutes longer or until cheese is melted. Let stand for 10 minutes before serving.

Easy Beef Pie

Ingredients

1 tablespoon vegetable oil
1/2 pound cubed beef chuck roast
1 cup red wine
1 (10.5 ounce) can beef gravy
1 (15 ounce) can mixed vegetables
2 (9 inch) pie crusts
1 egg white

Directions

Preheat oven to 350 degrees F (175 degrees C).

Heat oil in a medium saucepan over medium heat; saute the stew meat for 10 minutes, or until well browned on all sides. Reduce heat to low and add the red wine. Cover and simmer for 15 minutes, allowing the alcohol to cook off.

Remove cover and add the gravy and vegetables. Stir well and simmer for 10 more minutes. Pour mixture into one pastry shell. Cover with second pastry shell, sealing edges and cutting steam vents in top. Brush edges with egg white. Place pie on a baking sheet.

Bake at 350 degrees F (175 degrees C) for 30 to 45 minutes.

Rich, Easy, Old-Fashioned Chocolate Pudding

Ingredients

2 cups cold fat-free half-and-half
1/4 cup cornstarch
1 (11.5 ounce) package Ghirardelli 60% cocoa bittersweet chocolate chips
3 fluid ounces Amaretto liqueur (or rum)

Directions

In a medium saucepan, stir together 1 cup half and half and the cornstarch until smooth. Add remaining half and half. Over low heat, bring mixture to a simmer, stirring constantly to prevent sticking. Remove from heat.

Put chocolate and Amaretto in a small bowl; microwave on high 20 seconds. Stir until chips are mostly melted.

Return milk to low heat. Add chocolate; stir continuously, scraping pan, until thick.

Cool. Serve chilled or at room temperature.

Easy Chocolate Sherbet

Ingredients

cup sugar

3/4 cup unsweetened cocoa
powder

1/2 cups water

2 tablespoons amaretto (almond
flavored liqueur)

Directions

In a medium bowl, whisk together sugar, cocoa, water, and
amaretto until smooth.

Pour mixture into an ice cream freezer container, and follow the
manufacturer's instructions to freeze.

Easy Mac and Cheese Soup

Ingredients

1 (14 ounce) package uncooked macaroni and cheese
1 cup chopped broccoli
1/2 cup chopped onion
1 cup water
2 1/2 cups milk
1 (11 ounce) can condensed cream of Cheddar cheese soup
1 cup cubed cooked ham

Directions

Cook macaroni according to package directions; drain. Do not stir in the sauce.

In a medium saucepan, combine broccoli, onion and water. Bring to a boil and cook until broccoli is tender. Stir in macaroni, cheese mixture from package, milk, soup and ham. Return to a boil briefly. Serve hot.

CPSIA information can be obtained
at www.ICGtesting.com
Printed in the USA
LVHW101056220521
688045LV00021B/311